ETHIOPIC PARADIGMS

AARON M. BUTTS

ETHIOPIC PARADIGMS

A Summary of Classical Ethiopic (Gəʿəz)
Morphology

PEETERS

LEUVEN - PARIS - BRISTOL, CT

2022

A catalogue record for this book is available from the Library of Congress.

© Peeters, Bondgenotenlaan 153, B-3000 Leuven, Belgium - 2022
D/2022/0602/40
ISBN 978-90-429-4486-2
eISBN 978-90-429-4487-9

For Gene Gragg

TABLE OF CONTENTS

PREFACE

There has long been a need for a fresh collection of paradigms of Gəʿəz (Classical Ethiopic). This is largely a reflection of the current state of grammars available for this language. Over the past several decades, many students, especially in the English-speaking world, have learned Gəʿəz through T. O. Lambdin's *Introduction to Classical Ethiopic (Geʿez)* (Harvard Semitic Studies 24; Atlanta: Scholars Press, 1978). Its many strengths notwithstanding, one shortcoming of this textbook is that it does not include sufficient paradigms for reference: A paltry three pages at the end of the book are dedicated to paradigms. In addition, and equally problematically, Lambdin's *Introduction* does not employ the Gəʿəz script but instead transcription throughout. Similar shortcomings are found with J. Tropper's *Altäthiopisch. Grammatik des Geʿez mit Übungstexten und Glossar* (Elementa Linguarum Orientis 2; Münster: Ugarit-Verlag, 2002), which likewise has too few paradigms and again all in transcription. The situation is slightly improved in the recent English translation of Tropper's grammar by R. Hasselbach-Andee under the title *Classical Ethiopic. A Grammar of Geʿez* (Languages of the Ancient Near East 10; University Park: Eisenbrauns, 2021): The Gəʿəz script has happily been added throughout the main text, but unfortunately the collection of paradigms at the end still lacks the Gəʿəz script, and in addition it remains too meager.

Students learning from these textbooks must inevitably search elsewhere for a convenient collection of paradigms in the Gəʿəz script. Most students end up consulting one of several older grammars, including F. Praetorius's *Grammatica aethiopica* (Karlsruhe and Leipzig: H. Reuther, 1886) and M. Chaine, *Grammaire éthiopienne* (new ed.; Beirut: Imprimerie catholique, 1938). Recourse can of course also be made to what continues to be the standard reference grammar of Gəʿəz, even though it is woefully out of date and in need of replacement: A. Dillmann's *Grammatik der äthiopischen Sprache* (1st ed. Leipzig: T. O. Weigel, 1857; 2nd ed. Leipzig: C. H. Tauchnitz, 1899), the second edition of which, as enlarged and expanded by C. Bezold, was translated into English by J. A. Crichton under the title *Ethiopic Grammar* (London: Williams & Norgate, 1907). These grammars include helpful selections of paradigms in the Ethiopic script. They are not, however, always readily at hand for beginning students. In addition, these grammars only use the Gəʿəz script, never providing transcription. This leaves crucial grammatical information ambiguous, since the Gəʿəz script is undermarked in several ways, including that it does not mark consonantal gemination (i.e., doubling) and that it does not mark the distinction between the vowel ə and no vowel. Both of these features are phonemic in Gəʿəz, and recognizing them is crucial to an accurate analysis of the language. Thus, it is essential that students see the language *both* in Gəʿəz script—if nothing else, for the ease of reading—*and* in transcription, where certain ambiguous features of the script can be clarified. To date, there is no resource that accomplishes this double task. The present compendium aims to fill this void.

This compendium has been greatly improved over the course of a number of years by students in my Gəʿəz classes, first at Yale University and now at The Catholic University of America. These students have done everything from weeding out typos to offering more-far-reaching conceptual suggestions on the presentation of the material. I am grateful to these students without whose input this work would have been much less accurate and useful. I would also like to thank Jeremy Brown, Heath Dewrell, and Dawit Muluneh, who used this material in their own teaching and provided extensive feedback and corrections based on this, as well as Michael Hensley and Mehari Worku, who helped with the correction of the proofs.

One person's name often came to mind as I worked on this material over the years: Gene Gragg. Gene has devoted significant attention to analyzing the paradigms of Afroasiatic languages (including Gəʿəz) in the context of his Afroasiastic Morphological Archive (AAMA) project, which previously had the more comical acronym COMA, for Cushitic-Omotic Morphological Archive. In addition, even after his retirement, Gene was still willing to set aside time to read Gəʿəz texts with me when I was a beginning graduate student at the University of Chicago. And so it is to Gene that I dedicate this work as a small token of my appreciation.

Aaron Michael Butts
The Catholic University of America

ABBREVIATIONS

1	first-person
2	second-person
3	third-person
ACC	accusative
C	common (gender)
CNVRB	converb
F	feminine
IMPF	imperfect
IMPV	imperative
INF	infinitive
M	masculine
NON-ACC	non-accusative
PF	perfect
PL	plural
SG	singular
SUBJ	subjunctive

PARADIGMS

1. INDEPENDENT PERSONAL PRONOUNS

	SG		PL	
1.c	አነ	*ʾana*	ንሕነ	*nəḥna*
2.M	አንተ	*ʾanta*	አንተሙ	*ʾantəmu*
2.F	አንቲ	*ʾanti*	አንትን	*ʾantən*
3.M.NON-ACC	ውእቱ	*wəʾətu*	እሙንቱ	*ʾəmuntu*
3.M.ACC	ውእተ	*wəʾəta*		
3.F.NON-ACC	ይእቲ	*yəʾəti*	እማንቱ	*ʾəmāntu*
3.F.ACC	ይእተ	*yəʾəta*		

* ውእቶሙ *wəʾətomu* is also attested for 3.C.PL.
** ውእቶን *wəʾəton* is also occasionally found for 3.F.PL.

2. PRONOMINAL SUFFIXES ON CONSONANT-FINAL NOUNS

	NON-ACC noun		ACC noun	
1.C.SG	ሀገርየ	*hagarəya*	ሀገርየ	*hagarəya*
2.M.SG	ሀገርከ	*hagarəka*	ሀረከ	*hagaraka*
2.F.SG	ሀገርኪ	*hagarəki*	ሀረኪ	*hagaraki*
3.M.SG	ሀገሩ	*hagaru*	ሀገሮ	*hagaro*
3.F.SG	ሀገራ	*hagarā*	ሀገራ	*hagarā*
1.C.PL	ሀገርነ	*hagarəna*	ሀረነ	*hagarana*
2.M.PL	ሀገርከሙ	*hagarəkəmu*	ሀረከሙ	*hagarakəmu*
2.F.PL	ሀገርክን	*hagarəkən*	ሀረክን	*hagarakən*
3.M.PL	ሀገሮሙ	*hagaromu*	ሀገሮሙ	*hagaromu*
3.F.PL	ሀገሮን	*hagaron*	ሀገሮን	*hagaron*

3. Pronominal Suffixes on Singular Nouns Ending in -*i*

	NON-ACC noun		ACC noun	
1.C.SG	ጸሐፊየ	ṣaḥāfiya	ጸሐፊየ	ṣaḥāfiya
2.M.SG	ጸሐፊከ	ṣaḥāfika	ጸሐፊከ	ṣaḥāfeka
2.F.SG	ጸሐፊኪ	ṣaḥāfiki	ጸሐፊኪ	ṣaḥāfeki
3.M.SG	ጸሐፊሁ	ṣaḥāfihu	ጸሐፊሁ	ṣaḥāfihu
3.F.SG	ጸሐፊሃ	ṣaḥāfihā	ጸሐፊሃ	ṣaḥāfihā
1.C.PL	ጸሐፊነ	ṣaḥāfina	ጸሐፊነ	ṣaḥāfina
2.M.PL	ጸሐፊክሙ	ṣaḥāfikəmu	ጸሐፊክሙ	ṣaḥāfekəmu
2.F.PL	ጸሐፊክን	ṣaḥāfikən	ጸሐፊክን	ṣaḥāfekən
3.M.PL	ጸሐፊሆሙ	ṣaḥāfihomu	ጸሐፊሆሙ	ṣaḥāfihomu
3.F.PL	ጸሐፊሆን	ṣaḥāfihon	ጸሐፊሆን	ṣaḥāfihon

4. Pronominal Suffixes on Singular Nouns Ending in -*e*, -*ā*, and -*o*

	NON-ACC / ACC noun	
1.C.SG	አርዌየ	ʾarweya
2.M.SG	አርዌከ	ʾarweka
2.F.SG	አርዌኪ	ʾarweki
3.M.SG	አርዌሁ	ʾarwehu
3.F.SG	አርዌሃ	ʾarwehā
1.C.PL	አርዌነ	ʾarwena
2.M.PL	አርዌክሙ	ʾarwekəmu
2.F.PL	አርዌክን	ʾarwekən
3.M.PL	አርዌሆሙ	ʾarwehomu
3.F.PL	አርዌሆን	ʾarwehon

5. Pronominal Suffixes on Plural Nouns

	NON-ACC / ACC noun	
1.c.sg	አህጕሪየ / አህጕርየ	ʾahguriya / ʾahgurəya
2.m.sg	አህጕሪከ	ʾahgurika
2.f.sg	አህጕሪኪ / አህጕርኪ	ʾahguriki / ʾahgurəki
3.m.sg	አህጕሪሁ	ʾahgurihu
3.f.sg	አህጕሪሃ	ʾahgurihā
1.c.pl	አህጕሪነ	ʾahgurina
2.m.pl	አህጕሪከሙ	ʾahgurikəmu
2.f.pl	አህጕሪከን	ʾahgurikən
3.m.pl	አህጕሪሆሙ	ʾahgurihomu
3.f.pl	አህጕሪሆን	ʾahgurihon

6. Pronominal Suffixes on the 'Four Nouns'

	NON-ACC noun		ACC noun	
1.c.sg	አቡየ	ʾabuya	አባየ	ʾabāya
2.m.sg	አቡከ	ʾabuka	አባከ	ʾabāka
2.f.sg	አቡኪ	ʾabuki	አባኪ	ʾabāki
3.m.sg	አቡሁ	ʾabuhu	አባሁ	ʾabāhu
3.f.sg	አቡሃ	ʾabuhā	አባሃ	ʾabāhā
1.c.pl	አቡነ	ʾabuna	አባነ	ʾabāna
2.m.pl	አቡከሙ	ʾabukəmu	አባከሙ	ʾabākəmu
2.f.pl	አቡከን	ʾabukən	አባከን	ʾabākən
3.m.pl	አቡሆሙ	ʾabuhomu	አባሆሙ	ʾabāhomu
3.f.pl	አቡሆን	ʾabuhon	አባሆን	ʾabāhon

7. Pronominal Suffixes on እድ *ʾǝd* 'Hand'

	NON-ACC / ACC noun	
1.C.SG	እዴየ	*ʾǝdeya*
2.M.SG	እዴከ	*ʾǝdeka*
2.F.SG	እዴኪ	*ʾǝdeki*
3.M.SG	እዴሁ	*ʾǝdehu*
3.F.SG	እዴሃ	*ʾǝdehā*
1.C.PL	እዴነ	*ʾǝdena*
2.M.PL	እዴክሙ	*ʾǝdekǝmu*
2.F.PL	እዴክን	*ʾǝdekǝn*
3.M.PL	እዴሆሙ	*ʾǝdehomu*
3.F.PL	እዴሆን	*ʾǝdehon*

8. Object Pronominal Suffixes

See pp. 24–26 below.

9. First Series of 'Near' Demonstratives

	SG		PL	
M.NON-ACC	ዝ *zǝ*		እሉ	*ʾǝllu*
M.ACC	ዛ *za*			
F.NON-ACC / ACC	ዛ *zā*		እላ	*ʾǝllā*
			እሎን	*ʾǝllon*

10. SECOND SERIES OF 'NEAR' DEMONSTRATIVES

		SG		PL
M.NON-ACC	ዝንቱ	zəntu	እሎንቱ እሉንቱ	ʾəllontu ʾəlluntu
M.ACC	ዘንተ	zanta	እሎንተ እሉንተ	ʾəllonta ʾəllunta
F.NON-ACC	ዛቲ	zātti	እላንቱ እላንቲ	ʾəllāntu ʾəllānti
F.ACC	ዛተ	zātta	እላንተ	ʾəllānta

11. FIRST SERIES OF 'FAR' DEMONSTRATIVES

	SG		PL	
M.NON-ACC	ዝኩ	zə(k)ku		
M.ACC	ዝኰ	zə(k)kʷa	እልኩ	ʾəllə(k)ku
F.NON-ACC	እንተኩ	ʾəntə(k)ku		
F.ACC	እንተኰ	ʾəntə(k)kʷa		

12. SECOND SERIES OF 'FAR' DEMONSTRATIVES

	SG		PL	
M.NON-ACC	ዝክቱ ዝኵቱ	zəktu zəkʷtu	እልክቱ እልኵቱ	ʾəlləktu ʾəlləkʷtu
M.ACC	ዝክተ ዝኵተ	zəkta zəkʷta	እልክተ እልኵተ	ʾəlləkta ʾəlləkʷta
F.NON-ACC	እንታክቲ	ʾəntākti	እላክቱ	ʾəllāktu
F.ACC	እንታክተ	ʾəntākta	እላክተ	ʾəllākta

13. Relative Pronoun

	SG		PL	
M	ዘ	za-	እለ	ʾəlla
F	እንተ	ʾənta		

14. Interrogative Pronouns and Adjectives

	NON-ACC		ACC	
who?	መኑ	mannu	መነ	manna
what?	ምንት	mənt	ምንተ	mənta
which? (SG)	አይ	ʾayy	አየ	ʾayya
which? (PL)	አያት	ʾayyāt	አያተ	ʾayyāta

15. Interrogative Adverbs

where?	አይቴ	ʾayte
when?	ማእዜ	māʾze
how?	እፎ	ʾəffo
why?	ለምንት	lamənt
	በእንተ፡ምንት	baʾənta mənt

16. State Marking on Nouns

	absolute		construct	
ending in consonant	ንጉሥ	nəguś	ንጉሠ	nəguśa
ending in -i	ጸሐፊ	ṣaḥāfi	ጸሐፌ	ṣaḥāfe
ending in -e, -ā, -o	አርዌ	ʾarwe	አርዌ	ʾarwe

17. CASE MARKING ON NOUNS

	NON-ACC		ACC	
ending in consonant	ንጉሥ	nəguś	ንጉሠ	nəguśa
ending in -i	ጸሓፊ	ṣaḥāfi	ጸሓፌ	ṣaḥāfe
ending in -e, -ā, -o	አርዌ	ʔarwe	አርዌ	ʔarwe
proper noun	ዮሐንስ	yoḥannəs	ዮሐንሣ	yoḥannəshā[1]

[1] The unmarked (non-accusative) form also occurs for the accusative.

18. CARDINAL NUMBERS 1-10

	used with masculine nouns					used with feminine nouns				
	NON-ACC		ACC			NON-ACC		ACC		
1	አሐዱ	ʔaḥadu	አሐደ	ʔaḥada		አሐቲ	ʔaḥatti	አሐተ	ʔaḥatta	
2*	ክልኤቱ	kəlʔetu	ክልኤተ	kəlʔeta		ክልኤቲ	kəlʔeti	ክልኤተ	kəlʔeta	
3	ሠለስቱ	śalastu	ሠለስተ	śalasta		ሠላስ	śalās	ሠላሰ	śalāsa	
4	አርባዕቱ	ʔarbāʕtu	አርባዕተ	ʔarbāʕta		አርባዕ	ʔarbāʕ	አርባዐ	ʔarbāʕa	
5	ኀምስቱ	ḫaməstu	ኀምስተ	ḫaməsta		ኀምስ	ḫams	ኀምሰ	ḫamsa	
6	ስድስቱ	sədəstu	ስድስተ	sədəsta		ስሱ	səssu	ስሱ	səssu	
7	ሰብዐቱ	sabʕatu	ሰብዐተ	sabʕata		ሰብዑ	sabʕu			
	ሰባዕቱ	sabāʕtu	ሰባዕተ	sabāʕta		ሰብዕ	sabʕ	ሰብዑ	sabʕu	
						ስብዕ	səbʕ			
8	ሰመንቱ	samantu	ሰመንተ	samanta						
	ሰማንቱ	samāntu	ሰማንተ	samānta		ሰማኒ	samāni	ሰማኒ	samāni	
	ሰማኒቱ	samānitu	ሰማኒተ	samānita						
9	ትስዐቱ	təsʕatu	ትስዐተ	təsʕata		ትስዑ	təsʕu	ትስዑ	təsʕu	
	ተስዐቱ	tasʕatu	ተስዐተ	tasʕata		ተስዑ	tasʕu	ተስዑ	tasʕu	
	ተሳዕቱ	tasāʕtu	ተሳዕተ	tasāʕta						
10	ዐሠርቱ	ʕaśartu	ዐሠርተ	ʕaśarta		ዐሥሩ	ʕaśru	ዐሥሩ	ʕaśru	
						ዐሥር	ʕaśr	ዐሥረ	ʕaśra	

* For two, the form ክልኤ kəlʔe is also used with both masculine and feminine nouns regardless of case.

19. Strong Verb: Verbal Stems

		G-stem		D-stem		L-stem	
underived	PF	ቀተለ	ḳatala[1]	ቀተለ	ḳattala	ቃተለ	ḳātala
	IMPF	ይቀትል	yəḳattəl	ይቄትል	yəḳettəl	ይቃትል	yəḳāttəl
	SUBJ	ይቅትል	yəḳtəl[2]	ይቀትል	yəḳattəl	ይቃትል	yəḳātəl
	IMPV	ቅትል	ḳətəl[3]	ቀትል	ḳattəl	ቃትል	ḳātəl
	CNVRB	ቀቲሎ	ḳatilo	ቀቲሎ	ḳattilo	ቃቲሎ	ḳātilo
	INF	ቀቲል	ḳatil[4]	ቀትሎ(ት)	ḳattəlo(t)	ቃትሎ(ት)	ḳātəlo(t)
C-stem	PF	አቅተለ	ʾaḳtala	አቀተለ	ʾaḳattala	አቃተለ	ʾaḳātala
	IMPF	ያቀትል	yāḳattəl	ያቄትል	yāḳettəl	ያቃትል	yāḳāttəl
	SUBJ	ያቅትል	yāḳtəl	ያቀትል	yāḳattəl	ያቃትል	yāḳātəl
	IMPV	አቅትል	ʾaḳtəl	አቀትል	ʾaḳattəl	አቃትል	ʾaḳātəl
	CNVRB	አቅቲሎ	ʾaḳtilo	አቀቲሎ	ʾaḳattilo	አቃቲሎ	ʾaḳātilo
	INF	አቅትሎ(ት)	ʾaḳtəlo(t)	አቀትሎ(ት)	ʾaḳattəlo(t)	አቃትሎ(ት)	ʾaḳātəlo(t)
T-stem	PF	ተቀተለ	taḳatala[5]	ተቀተለ	taḳattala	ተቃተለ	taḳātala
	IMPF	ይትቀተል	yətḳattal	ይትቄተል	yətḳettal	ይትቃተል	yətḳāttal
	SUBJ	ይትቀተል	yətḳatal	ይትቀተል	yətḳattal	ይትቃተል	yətḳātal
	IMPV	ተቀተል	taḳatal	ተቀተል	taḳattal	ተቃተል	taḳātal
	CNVRB	ተቀቲሎ	taḳatilo	ተቀቲሎ	taḳattilo	ተቃቲሎ	taḳātilo
	INF	ተቀትሎ(ት)	taḳatəlo(t)	ተቀትሎ(ት)	taḳattəlo(t)	ተቃትሎ(ት)	taḳātəlo(t)
CT-stem	PF	አስተቅተለ	ʾastaḳtala[6]	አስተቀተለ	ʾastaḳattala	አስተቃተለ	ʾastaḳātala
	IMPF	ያስተቀትል	yāstaḳattəl	ያስተቄትል	yāstaḳettəl	ያስተቃትል	yāstaḳāttəl
	SUBJ	ያስተቅትል	yāstaḳtəl	ያስተቀትል	yāstaḳattəl	ያስተቃትል	yāstaḳātəl
	IMPV	አስተቅትል	ʾastaḳtəl	አስተቀትል	ʾastaḳattəl	አስተቃትል	ʾastaḳātəl
	CNVRB	አስተቅቲሎ	ʾastaḳtilo	አስተቀቲሎ	ʾastaḳattilo	አስተቃቲሎ	ʾastaḳātilo
	INF	አስተቅትሎ(ት)	ʾastaḳtəlo(t)	አስተቀትሎ(ት)	ʾastaḳattəlo(t)	አስተቃትሎ(ት)	ʾastaḳātəlo(t)

* The root ḳtl is used for illustration only; it is not attested in all stems.
[1] B-type ገብረ gabra.
[2] B-type ይግበር yəgbar.
[3] B-type ግበር gəbar.
[4] Also ቀቲሎት ḳatilot.
[5] Also ተቀትለ taḳatla.
[6] Also አስተቀተለ ʾastaḳatala.

20. STRONG VERB: G-STEM PERFECT

	SG				PL			
	A-type		B-type		A-type		B-type	
1.C	ነገርኩ	nagarku	ገበርኩ	gabarku	ነገርነ	nagarna	ገበርነ	gabarna
2.M	ነገርከ	nagarka	ገበርከ	gabarka	ነገርክሙ	nagarkəmu	ገበርክሙ	gabarkəmu
2.F	ነገርኪ	nagarki	ገበርኪ	gabarki	ነገርክን	nagarkən	ገበርክን	gabarkən
3.M	ነገረ	nagara	ገብረ	gabra	ነገሩ	nagaru	ገብሩ	gabru
3.F	ነገረት	nagarat	ገብረት	gabrat	ነገራ	nagarā	ገብራ	gabrā

21. STRONG VERB: G-STEM IMPERFECT

	SG		PL	
1.C	እነግር	ʾənaggər	ንነግር	nənaggər
2.M	ትነግር	tənaggər	ትነግሩ	tənaggəru
2.F	ትነግሪ	tənaggəri	ትነግራ	tənaggərā
3.M	ይነግር	yənaggər	ይነግሩ	yənaggəru
3.F	ትነግር	tənaggər	ይነግራ	yənaggərā

22. STRONG VERB: G-STEM SUBJUNCTIVE

	SG				PL			
	A-type		B-type		A-type		B-type	
1.C	እንግር	ʾəngər	እግብር	ʾəgbar	ንንግር	nəngər	ንግብር	nəgbar
2.M	ትንግር	təngər	ትግብር	təgbar	ትንግሩ	təngəru	ትግብሩ	təgbaru
2.F	ትንግሪ	təngəri	ትግብሪ	təgbari	ትንግራ	təngərā	ትግብራ	təgbarā
3.M	ይንግር	yəngər	ይግብር	yəgbar	ይንግሩ	yəngəru	ይግብሩ	yəgbaru
3.F	ትንግር	təngər	ትግብር	təgbar	ይንግራ	yəngərā	ይግብራ	yəgbarā

23. STRONG VERB: G-STEM IMPERATIVE

	SG				PL			
	A-type		B-type		A-type		B-type	
2.M	ንግር	nəgər	ግብር	gəbar	ንግሩ	nəgəru	ግብሩ	gəbaru
2.F	ንግሪ	nəgəri	ግብሪ	gəbari	ንግራ	nəgərā	ግብራ	gəbarā

24. STRONG VERB: G-STEM CONVERB

	SG		PL	
1.C	ነጊርየ	nagirəya	ነጊረነ	nagirana
2.M	ነጊረከ	nagiraka	ነጊረክሙ	nagirakəmu
2.F	ነጊረኪ	nagiraki	ነጊረክን	nagirakən
3.M	ነጊሮ	nagiro	ነጊሮሙ	nagiromu
3.F	ነጊራ	nagirā	ነጊሮን	nagiron

25. II=III: Verbal Stems

		G-stem		D-stem		L-stem
underived	PF	ነበበ	nababa[1]	ነበበ	nabbaba	ናበበ	nābaba
	IMPF	ይነብብ	yənabbəb	ይኔብብ	yənebbəb	ይናብብ	yənābbəb
	SUBJ	ይንብብ	yənbəb[2]	ይነብብ	yənabbəb	ይናብብ	yənābəb
	IMPV	ንብብ	nəbəb[3]	ነብብ	nabbəb	ናብብ	nābəb
	CNVRB	ነቢቦ	nabibo	ነቢቦ	nabbibo	ናቢቦ	nābibo
	INF	ነቢብ	nabib[4]	ነብቦ(ት)	nabbəbo(t)	ናብቦ(ት)	nābəbo(t)
C-stem	PF	አንበበ	ʾanbaba	አነበበ	ʾanabbaba	አናበበ	ʾanābaba
	IMPF	ያነብብ	yānabbəb	ያኔብብ	yānebbəb	ያናብብ	yānābbəb
	SUBJ	ያንብብ	yānbəb	ያነብብ	yānabbəb	ያናብብ	yānābəb
	IMPV	አንብብ	ʾanbəb	አነብብ	ʾanabbəb	አናብብ	ʾanābəb
	CNVRB	አንቢቦ	ʾanbibo	አነቢቦ	ʾanabbibo	አናቢቦ	ʾanābibo
	INF	አንበቦ(ት)	ʾanbəbo(t)	አነብቦ(ት)	ʾanabbəbo(t)	አናብቦ(ት)	ʾanābəbo(t)
T-stem	PF	ተነበ	tanabba[5]	ተነበበ	tanabbaba	ተናበበ	tanābaba
	IMPF	ይትነበብ	yətnabbab	ይትኔብብ	yətnebbab	ይትናብብ	yətnābbab
	SUBJ	ይትነበብ	yətnabab	ይትነበብ	yətnabbab	ይትናብብ	yətnābab
	IMPV	ተነበብ	tanabab	ተነበብ	tanabbab	ተናበብ	tanābab
	CNVRB	ተነቢቦ	tanabibo	ተነቢቦ	tanabbibo	ተናቢቦ	tanābibo
	INF	ተነብቦ(ት)	tanabəbo(t)	ተነብቦ(ት)	tanabbəbo(t)	ተናብቦ(ት)	tanābəbo(t)
CT-stem	PF	አስተነበበ	ʾastanababa	አስተነበበ	ʾastanabbaba	አስተናበበ	ʾastanābaba
	IMPF	ያስተነብብ	yāstanabbəb	ያስተኔብብ	yāstanebbəb	ያስተናብብ	yāstanābbəb
	SUBJ	ያስተንብብ	yāstanbəb	ያስተነብብ	yāstanabbəb	ያስተናብብ	yāstanābəb
	IMPV	አስተንብብ	ʾastanbəb	አስተነብብ	ʾastanabbəb	አስተናብብ	ʾastanābəb
	CNVRB	አስተንቢቦ	ʾastanbibo	አስተነቢቦ	ʾastanabbibo	አስተናቢቦ	ʾastanābibo
	INF	አስተንብቦ(ት)	ʾastanbəbo(t)	አስተነብቦ(ት)	ʾastanabbəbo(t)	አስተናብቦ(ት)	ʾastanābəbo(t)

* The root *nbb* is used for illustration only; it is not attested in all stems.
[1] B-type ነደ *nadda*.
[2] B-type ይንደድ *yəndad*.
[3] B-type ንደድ *nədad*.
[4] Also ነቢቦት *nabibot*.
[5] Also ተነበበ *tanababa*.

26. II=III (B-TYPE): G-STEM PERFECT

	SG		PL	
1.C	ነደድኩ	nadadku	ነደድነ	nadadna
2.M	ነደድከ	nadadka	ነደድክሙ	nadadkəmu
2.F	ነደድኪ	nadadki	ነደድክን	nadadkən
3.M	ነደ	nadda	ነዱ	naddu
3.F	ነደት	naddat	ነዳ	naddā

27. II=III: G-STEM IMPERFECT

	SG			PL			
1.C	እነብብ	ʾənabbəb		ንነብብ		nənabbəb	
2.M	ትነብብ	tənabbəb		ትነብቡ	tənabbəbu or	ትነቡ	tənabbu
2.F	ትነብቢ	tənabbəbi or	ትነቢ tənabbi	ትነብባ	tənabbəbā or	ትነባ	tənabbā
3.M	ይነብብ	yənabbəb		ይነብቡ	yənabbəbu or	ይነቡ	yənabbu
3.F	ትነብብ	tənabbəb		ይነብባ	yənabbəbā or	ይነባ	yənabbā

28. II=III: G-STEM IMPERATIVE

	SG			PL			
2.M	ንብብ	nəbəb		ንብቡ	nəbəbu or	ንቡ	nəbbu
2.F	ንብቢ	nəbəbi or	ንቢ nəbbi	ንብባ	nəbəbā or	ንባ	nəbbā

29. I=*w/y*: Verbal Stems

		G-stem		D-stem		L-stem	
underived	PF	ወረደ	warada[1]	ወረደ	warrada		
	IMPF	ይወርድ	yəwarrəd[2]	ይዌርድ	yəwerrəd		
	SUBJ	ይረድ	yərad[3]	ይወርድ	yəwarrəd		
	IMPV	ረድ	rad[4]	ወርድ	warrəd		
	CNVRB	ወሪዶ	warido	ወሪዶ	warrido		
	INF	ወሪድ	warid[5]	ወርዶ(ት)	warrədo(t)		
C-stem	PF	አውረደ	ʾawrada	አወረደ	ʾawarrada		
	IMPF	ያወርድ	yāwarrəd	ያዌርድ	yāwerrəd		
	SUBJ	ያውርድ	yāwrəd	ያወርድ	yāwarrəd		
	IMPV	አውርድ	ʾawrəd	አወርድ	ʾawarrəd		
	CNVRB	አውሪዶ	ʾawrido	አወሪዶ	ʾawarrido		
	INF	አውርዶ(ት)	ʾawrədo(t)	አወርዶ(ት)	ʾawarrədo(t)		
T-stem	PF	ተወርደ	tawarda	ተወረደ	tawarrada	ተዋረደ	tawārada
	IMPF	ይትወርድ	yətwarrad	ይትዌርድ	yətwerrad	ይትዋረድ	yətwārrad
	SUBJ	ይትወረድ	yətwarad	ይትወረድ	yətwarrad	ይትዋረድ	yətwārad
	IMPV	ተወረድ	tawarad	ተወረድ	tawarrad	ተዋረድ	tawārad
	CNVRB	ተወሪዶ	tawarido	ተወሪዶ	tawarrido	ተዋሪዶ	tawārido
	INF	ተወርዶ(ት)	tawarədo(t)	ተወርዶ(ት)	tawarrədo(t)	ተዋርዶ(ት)	tawārədo(t)
CT-stem	PF	አስተውረደ	ʾastawrada	አስተወረደ	ʾastawarrada	አስተዋረደ	ʾastawārada
	IMPF	ያስተወርድ	yāstawarrəd	ያስተዌርድ	yāstawerrəd	ያስተዋርድ	yāstawārrəd
	SUBJ	ያስተውርድ	yāstawrəd	ያስተወርድ	yāstawarrəd	ያስተዋረድ	yāstawārəd
	IMPV	አስተውርድ	ʾastawrəd	አስተወርድ	ʾastawarrəd	አስተዋርድ	ʾastawārəd
	CNVRB	አስተውሪዶ	ʾastawrido	አስተወሪዶ	ʾastawarrido	አስተዋሪዶ	ʾastawārido
	INF	አስተውርዶ(ት)	ʾastawrədo(t)	አስተወርዶ(ት)	ʾastawarrədo(t)	አስተዋርዶ(ት)	ʾastawārədo(t)

* The root *wrd* is used for illustration only; it is not attested in all stems.

[1] B-type ወድቀ *wadḵa*.

[2] Note also the irregular form ይሁብ *yəhub*.

[3] Alternative forms include ይውስድ *yəwsəd* (especially for A-type) and more rarely ይስድ *yəsəd* and ይውሐዝ *yəwḥaz*. Note also the irregular form የሀብ *yahab*.

[4] Alternative forms include ውጠን *wəṭən* (especially for A-type) and more rarely ስድ *səd*.

[5] Also ወሪዶት *waridot*.

30. II=*W/Y*: VERBAL STEMS

		G-stem		D-stem		L-stem	
underived	PF	ቆመ	koma[1]	ቀወመ	kawwama		
	IMPF	ይቀው·ም	yəkawwəm	ይቄው·ም	yəkewwəm		
	SUBJ	ይቁም	yəkum[2]	ይቀው·ም	yəkawwəm		
	IMPV	ቁም	kum[3]	ቀው·ም	kawwəm		
	CNVRB	ቀዊም	kawimo[4]	ቀዊም	kawwimo		
	INF	ቀዊም	kawim[5]	ቀው·ም(ት)	kawwəmo(t)		
C-stem	PF	አቆመ	ʾakoma[6]	አቀወመ	ʾakawwama		
	IMPF	ያቀው·ም	yākawwəm	ያቄው·ም	yākewwəm		
	SUBJ	ያቁም	yākum[7]	ያቀው·ም	yākawwəm		
	IMPV	አቁም	ʾakum[8]	አቀው·ም	ʾakawwəm		
	CNVRB	አቅዊም	ʾakwimo	አቀዊም	ʾakawwimo		
	INF	አቀው·ም(ት)	ʾakwəmo(t)	አቀው·ም(ት)	ʾakawwəmo(t)		
T-stem	PF	ተቀው·መ	takawma[9]	ተቀወመ	takawwama	ተቃወመ	takāwama
	IMPF	ይትቀወም	yətkawwam	ይትቄወም	yətkewwam	ይትቃወም	yətkāwwam
	SUBJ	ይትቀወም	yətkawam	ይትቀወም	yətkawwam	ይትቃወም	yətkāwam
	IMPV	ተቀወም	takawam	ተቀወም	takawwam	ተቃወም	takāwam
	CNVRB	ተቀዊም	takawimo	ተቀዊም	takawwimo	ተቃዊም	takāwimo
	INF	ተቀው·ም(ት)	takawəmo(t)	ተቀው·ም(ት)	takawwəmo(t)	ተቃው·ም(ት)	takāwəmo(t)
CT-stem	PF					አስተቃወመ	ʾastakāwama
	IMPF					ያስተቃው·ም	yāstakāwwəm
	SUBJ					ያስተቃው·ም	yāstakāwəm
	IMPV					አስተቃው·ም	ʾastakāwəm
	CNVRB					አስተቃዊም	ʾastakāwimo
	INF					አስተቃው·ም(ት)	ʾastakāwəmo(t)

* The root *qwm* is used for illustration only; it is not attested in all stems.
** Unless otherwise noted, for II-*y*, simply change *w* to *y*.
[1] II-*y* is ሢመ *śema*.
[2] Also ይሖር *yəhor* and more rarely ይባእ *yəbāʾ*. II-*y* is ይሢም *yəśim*.
[3] Also ሖር *hor* and more rarely ባእ *bāʾ*. II-*y* is ሢም *śim*.
[4] Also ቀው·ም *kawəmo*.
[5] Also ቀው·ም *kawəm* as well as ቀዊሞት *kawimot* and ቀው·ሞት *kawəmot*.
[6] Also አቀመ *ʾakama*. II-*y* is አኪደ *ʾakeda*.
[7] Also ያቅም *yākəm*. II-*y* is ያኪድ *yākid* (rarely ያክድ *yākəd*).
[8] Also አቅም *ʾakəm*. II-*y* is አኪድ *ʾakid* (rarely አክድ *ʾakəd*).
[9] Also ተቀወመ *takawama*.

31. III=w: VERBAL STEMS

		G-stem		D-stem		L-stem
underived	PF	ገለወ	galawa[1]	ገለወ	gallawa	ጋለወ	gālawa
	IMPF	ይገሉ	yəgallu	ይጌሉ	yəgellu	ይጋሉ	yəgāllu
	SUBJ	ይግሉ	yəglu[2]	ይገሉ	yəgallu	ይጋሉ	yəgālu
	IMPV	ግሉ	gəlu[3]	ገሉ	gallu	ጋሉ	gālu
	CNVRB	ገሊፀ	galiwo	ገሊፀ	galliwo	ጋሊፀ	gāliwo
	INF	ገሊው·	galiw[4]	ገልፀ(ት)	gallǝwo(t)	ጋልፀ(ት)	gālǝwo(t)
C-stem	PF	አግለወ	ʾaglawa	አገለወ	ʾagallawa	አጋለወ	ʾagālawa
	IMPF	ያገሉ	yāgallu	ያጌሉ	yāgellu	ያጋሉ	yāgāllu
	SUBJ	ያግሉ	yāglu	ያገሉ	yāgallu	ያጋሉ	yāgālu
	IMPV	አግሉ	ʾaglu	አገሉ	ʾagallu	አጋሉ	ʾagālu
	CNVRB	አግሊፀ	ʾagliwo	አገሊፀ	ʾagalliwo	አጋሊፀ	ʾagāliwo
	INF	አግልፀ(ት)	ʾaglǝwo(t)	አገልፀ(ት)	ʾagallǝwo(t)	አጋልፀ(ት)	ʾagālǝwo(t)
T-stem	PF	ተገለወ	tagalwa[5]	ተገለወ	tagallawa	ተጋለወ	tagālawa
	IMPF	ይትገለው·	yətgallaw	ይትጌለው·	yətgellaw	ይትጋለው·	yətgāllaw
	SUBJ	ይትገለው·	yətgalaw	ይትገለው·	yətgallaw	ይትጋለው·	yətgālaw
	IMPV	ተገለው·	tagalaw	ተገለው·	tagallaw	ተጋለው·	tagālaw
	CNVRB	ተገሊፀ	tagaliwo	ተገሊፀ	tagalliwo	ተጋሊፀ	tagāliwo
	INF	ተገልፀ(ት)	tagalǝwo(t)	ተገልፀ(ት)	tagallǝwo(t)	ተጋልፀ(ት)	tagālǝwo(t)
CT-stem	PF	አስተግለወ	ʾastaglawa[6]	አስተገለወ	ʾastagallawa	አስተጋለወ	ʾastagālawa
	IMPF	ያስተገሉ	yāstagallu	ያስተጌሉ	yāstagellu	ያስተጋሉ	yāstagāllu
	SUBJ	ያስተግሉ	yāstaglu	ያስተገሉ	yāstagallu	ያስተጋሉ	yāstagālu
	IMPV	አስተግሉ	ʾastaglu	አስተገሉ	ʾastagallu	አስተጋሉ	ʾastagālu
	CNVRB	አስተግሊፀ	ʾastagliwo	አስተገሊፀ	ʾastagalliwo	አስተጋሊፀ	ʾastagāliwo
	INF	አስተግልፀ(ት)	ʾastaglǝwo(t)	አስተገልፀ(ት)	ʾastagallǝwo(t)	አስተጋልፀ(ት)	ʾastagālǝwo(t)

* The root *glw* is used for illustration only; it is not attested in all stems.
** All forms ending in -*aw* can optionally contract to -*o* (this is not indicated).
[1] B-type ፈትወ *fatwa*.
[2] B-type ይፍተው· *yǝftaw*.
[3] B-type ፍተው· *fǝtaw*.
[4] Also ገሊፀት *galiwot*.
[5] Also ተገለወ *tagalawa*.
[6] Also አስተገለወ *ʾastagalawa*.

32. III=w: G-Stem Perfect

	SG			PL		
1.c	ገለውኩ	galawku or	ገሎኩ galoku	ገለውነ	galawna or	ገሎነ galona
2.m	ገለውከ	galawka or	ገሎከ galoka	ገለውክሙ	galawkəmu or	ገሎክሙ galokəmu
2.f	ገለውኪ.	galawki or	ገሎኪ. galoki	ገለውክን	galawkən or	ገሎክን galokən
3.m		ገለወ	galawa		ገለዉ.	galawu
3.f		ገለወት	galawat		ገለዋ	galawā

33. III=w: G-Stem Imperfect

		SG		PL
1.c	እገሉ	ʾəgallu	ንገሉ	nəgallu
2.m	ትገሉ	təgallu	ትገልዉ.	təgalləwu
2.f	ትገልዊ	təgalləwi	ትገልዋ	təgalləwā
3.m	ይገሉ	yəgallu	ይገልዉ.	yəgalləwu
3.f	ትገሉ	təgallu	ይገልዋ	yəgalləwā

34. III=w: G-Stem Subjunctive

		SG		PL
1.c	እግሉ	ʾəglu	ንግሉ	nəglu
2.m	ትግሉ	təglu	ትግልዉ.	təgləwu
2.f	ትግልዊ	təgləwi	ትግልዋ	təgləwā
3.m	ይግሉ	yəglu	ይግልዉ.	yəgləwu
3.f	ትግሉ	təglu	ይግልዋ	yəgləwā

35. III=Y: VERBAL STEMS

		G-stem		D-stem		L-stem	
underived	PF	በከየ	bakaya[1]	በከየ	bakkaya	ባከየ	bākaya
	IMPF	ይበኪ	yəbakki	ይቤኪ	yəbekki	ይባኪ	yəbākki
	SUBJ	ይብኪ	yəbki[2]	ይበኪ	yəbakki	ይባኪ	yəbāki
	IMPV	ብኪ	bəki[3]	በኪ	bakki	ባኪ	bāki
	CNVRB	በኪዮ	bakiyo[4]	በኪዮ	bakkiyo	ባኪዮ	bākiyo
	INF	በኪይ	bakiy[5]	በከዮ(ት)	bakkəyo(t)	ባከዮ(ት)	bākəyo(t)
C-stem	PF	አበከየ	ʾabkaya	አበከየ	ʾabakkaya	አባከየ	ʾabākaya
	IMPF	ያበኪ	yābakki	ያቤኪ	yābekki	ያባኪ	yābākki
	SUBJ	ያብኪ	yābki	ያበኪ	yābakki	ያባኪ	yābāki
	IMPV	አብኪ	ʾabki	አበኪ	ʾabakki	አባኪ	ʾabāki
	CNVRB	አብኪዮ	ʾabkiyo	አበኪዮ	ʾabakkiyo	አባኪዮ	ʾabākiyo
	INF	አብከዮ(ት)	ʾabkəyo(t)	አበከዮ(ት)	ʾabakkəyo(t)	አባከዮ(ት)	ʾabākəyo(t)
T-stem	PF	ተበከየ	tabakya[6]	ተበከየ	tabakkaya	ተባከየ	tabākaya
	IMPF	ይትበከይ	yətbakkay	ይትቤከይ	yətbekkay	ይትባከይ	yətbākkay
	SUBJ	ይትበከይ	yətbakay	ይትበከይ	yətbakkay	ይትባከይ	yətbākay
	IMPV	ተበከይ	tabakay	ተበከይ	tabakkay	ተባከይ	tabākay
	CNVRB	ተበኪዮ	tabakiyo	ተበኪዮ	tabakkiyo	ተባኪዮ	tabākiyo
	INF	ተበከዮ(ት)	tabakəyo(t)	ተበከዮ(ት)	tabakkəyo(t)	ተባከዮ(ት)	tabākəyo(t)
CT-stem	PF	አስተብከየ	ʾastabkaya[7]	አስተበከየ	ʾastabakkaya	አስተባከየ	ʾastabākaya
	IMPF	ያስተብኪ	yāstabakki	ያስተቤኪ	yāstabekki	ያስተባኪ	yāstabākki
	SUBJ	ያስተብኪ	yāstabki	ያስተበኪ	yāstabakki	ያስተባኪ	yāstabāki
	IMPV	አስተብኪ	ʾastabki	አስተበኪ	ʾastabakki	አስተባኪ	ʾastabāki
	CNVRB	አስተብኪዮ	ʾastabkiyo	አስተበኪዮ	ʾastabakkiyo	አስተባኪዮ	ʾastabākiyo
	INF	አስተብከዮ(ት)	ʾastabkəyo(t)	አስተበከዮ(ት)	ʾastabakkəyo(t)	አስተባከዮ(ት)	ʾastabākəyo(t)

* The root *bky* is used for illustration only; it is not attested in all stems.
** Rarely, forms ending in *-ay* are contracted to *-e*.

[1] B-type ሰትየ *satya*.
[2] B-type ይስተይ *yəstay*.
[3] B-type ስተይ *sətay*.
[4] Also በከዮ *bakəyo*.
[5] Also በከይ *bakəy* as well as በኪዮት *bakiyot* and በከዮት *bakəyot*.
[6] Also ተበከየ *tabakaya*.
[7] Also አስተበከየ *ʾastabakaya*.

36. III=Y: G-Stem Perfect

	SG				PL			
1.C	በከይኩ	*bakayku*	or	በኬኩ *bakeku*	በከይነ	*bakayna*	or	በኬነ *bakena*
2.M	በከይከ	*bakayka*	or	በኬከ *bakeka*	በከይክሙ	*bakaykəmu*	or	በኬክሙ *bakekəmu*
2.F	በከይኪ	*bakayki*	or	በኬኪ *bakeki*	በከይክን	*bakaykən*	or	በኬክን *bakekən*
3.M			በከየ	*bakaya*			በከዩ	*bakayu*
3.F			በከየት	*bakayat*			በከያ	*bakayā*

* The forms with *e* are rare.

37. III=Y: G-Stem Imperfect

	SG		PL	
1.C	እበኪ	*ʾəbakki*	ንበኪ	*nəbakki*
2.M	ትበኪ	*təbakki*	ትበከዩ	*təbakkəyu*
2.F	ትበከዪ	*təbakkəyi*	ትበከያ	*təbakkəyā*
3.M	ይበኪ	*yəbakki*	ይበከዩ	*yəbakkəyu*
3.F	ትበኪ	*təbakki*	ይበከያ	*yəbakkəyā*

38. III=Y: G-Stem Subjunctive

	SG		PL	
1.C	እብኪ	*ʾəbki*	ንብኪ	*nəbki*
2.M	ትብኪ	*təbki*	ትብከዩ	*təbkəyu*
2.F	ትብከዪ	*təbkəyi*	ትብከያ	*təbkəyā*
3.M	ይብኪ	*yəbki*	ይብከዩ	*yəbkəyu*
3.F	ትብኪ	*təbki*	ይብከያ	*yəbkəyā*

39. I=Guttural: Verbal Stems

		G-stem		D-stem		L-stem	
underived	PF	አሰረ	ʾasara[1]	አሰረ	ʾassara		
	IMPF	የአስር	yaʾassər	ይሔስር	yəʾessər		
	SUBJ	ይእስር	yəʾsər[2]	የአስር	yaʾassər		
	IMPV	እስር	ʾəsər[3]	አስር	ʾassər		
	CNVRB	አሲሮ	ʾasiro	አሲሮ	ʾassiro		
	INF	አሲር	ʾasir[4]	አስሮ(ት)	ʾassaro(t)		
C-stem	PF	አእሰረ	ʾaʾsara	አአሰረ	ʾaʾassara		
	IMPF	ያአስር	yāʾassər[5]	ያሔስር	yāʾessər		
	SUBJ	ያእስር	yāʾsər	ያአስር	yāʾassər		
	IMPV	አእስር	ʾaʾsər	አአስር	ʾaʾassər		
	CNVRB	አእሲሮ	ʾaʾsiro	አአሲሮ	ʾaʾassiro		
	INF	አእስሮ(ት)	ʾaʾsəro(t)	አአስሮ(ት)	ʾaʾassaro(t)		
T-stem	PF	ተአስረ	taʾasra[6]	ተአሰረ	taʾassara	ተአሰረ	taʾāsara
	IMPF	ይትአስር	yətʾassar	ይትሔስር	yətʾessar	ይትአስር	yətʾāssar
	SUBJ	ይትአስር	yətʾasar	ይትአስር	yətʾassar	ይትአስር	yətʾāsar
	IMPV	ተአስር	taʾasar	ተአስር	taʾassar	ተአስር	taʾāsar
	CNVRB	ተአሲሮ	taʾasiro	ተአሲሮ	taʾassiro	ተአሲሮ	taʾāsiro
	INF	ተአስሮ(ት)	taʾasəro(t)	ተአስሮ(ት)	taʾassaro(t)	ተአስሮ(ት)	taʾāsəro(t)
CT-stem	PF	አስተአሰረ	ʾastaʾasara[7]	አስተአሰረ	ʾastaʾassara	አስተአሰረ	ʾastaʾāsara
	IMPF	ያስተአስር	yāstaʾassar	ያስተሔስር	yāstaʾessar	ያስተአስር	yāstaʾāssar
	SUBJ	ያስታእስር	yāstāʾsər	ያስተአስር	yāstaʾassar	ያስተአስር	yāstaʾāsər
	IMPV	አስታእስር	ʾastāʾsər	አስተአስር	ʾastaʾassar	አስተአስር	ʾastaʾāsar
	CNVRB	አስታእሲሮ	ʾastāʾsiro	አስተአሲሮ	ʾastaʾassiro	አስተአሲሮ	ʾastaʾāsiro
	INF	አስታእስር(ት)	ʾastāʾsəro(t)	አስተአስር(ት)	ʾastaʾassaro(t)	አስተአስር(ት)	ʾastaʾāsəro(t)

* The root ʾsr is used for illustration only; it is not attested in all stems.

[1] B-type አምነ ʾamna.
[2] B-type ይእመን yəʾman.
[3] B-type እመን ʾəman.
[4] Also አሲሮት ʾasirot.
[5] Also የአስር yaʾassər.
[6] Also ተአሰረ taʾasara.
[7] Also አስታእሰረ ʾastāʾsara.

40. II=Guttural: Verbal Stems

		G-stem		D-stem		L-stem	
underived	PF	ለአከ	laʾaka[1]	ለአከ	laⁿaka	ላአከ	lāʾaka
	IMPF	ይልአክ	yəlaⁿək	ይሌአክ	yəleⁿək	ይላአክ	yəlāⁿək
	SUBJ	ይልአክ	yəlʾak[2]	ይልአክ	yəlaⁿək	ይላአክ	yəlāʾək
	IMPV	ለአክ	laʾak[3]	ልአክ	ləⁿək	ላአክ	lāʾək
	CNVRB	ልኢኮ	ləʾiko	ልኢኮ	ləⁿiko	ላኢኮ	lāʾiko
	INF	ልኢክ	ləʾik[4]	ልአኮ(ት)	ləⁿako(t)	ላአኮ(ት)	lāʾako(t)
C-stem	PF	አልአከ	ʾalʾaka	አለአከ	ʾalaⁿaka[7]	አላአከ	ʾalāʾaka
	IMPF	ያልአክ	yālaⁿək	ያሌአክ	yāleⁿək	ያላአክ	yālāⁿək
	SUBJ	ያልአክ	yālʾək	ያልአክ	yālaⁿək	ያላአክ	yālāʾək
	IMPV	አልአክ	ʾalʾək	አልአክ	ʾalaⁿək	አላአክ	ʾalāʾək
	CNVRB	አልኢኮ	ʾalʾiko	አልኢኮ	ʾalaⁿiko	አላኢኮ	ʾalāʾiko
	INF	አልአኮ(ት)	ʾalʾako(t)	አልአኮ(ት)	ʾalaⁿako(t)	አላአኮ(ት)	ʾalāʾako(t)
T-stem	PF	ተለአከ	talaʾka[5]	ተለአከ	talaⁿaka[8]	ተላአከ	talāʾaka
	IMPF	ይትለአክ	yətlaⁿak	ይትሌአክ	yətleⁿak	ይትላአክ	yətlāⁿak
	SUBJ	ይትለአክ	yətlaʾak	ይትለአክ	yətlaⁿak	ይትላአክ	yətlāʾak
	IMPV	ተለአክ	talaʾak	ተለአክ	talaⁿak	ተላአክ	talāʾak
	CNVRB	ተልኢኮ	talaʾiko	ተልኢኮ	talaⁿiko	ተላኢኮ	talāʾiko
	INF	ተልአኮ(ት)	talaʾako(t)	ተልአኮ(ት)	talaⁿako(t)	ተላአኮ(ት)	talāʾako(t)
CT-stem	PF	አስተልአከ	ʾastalʾaka[6]			አስተላአከ	ʾastalāʾaka
	IMPF	ያስተልአክ	yāstalaⁿək			ያስተላአክ	yāstalāⁿək
	SUBJ	ያስተልአክ	yāstalʾək			ያስተላአክ	yāstalāʾək
	IMPV	አስተልአክ	ʾastalʾək			አስተላአክ	ʾastalāʾək
	CNVRB	አስተልኢኮ	ʾastalʾiko			አስተላኢኮ	ʾastalāʾiko
	INF	አስተልአኮ(ት)	ʾastalʾako(t)			አስተላአኮ(ት)	ʾastalāʾako(t)

* The root *lʾk* is used for illustration only; it is not attested in all stems.

[1] B-type ለህቀ *ləhḳa*.
[2] B-type is the same, i.e., ይልህቅ *yəlhaḳ*.
[3] B-type is the same, i.e., ለህቅ *lahaḳ*.
[4] Also ልኢኮት *ləʾikot*.
[5] Also ተለአከ *talaʾaka*.
[6] Also አስተለአከ *ʾastalaʾaka*.
[7] Also አልአከ *ʾalʾaka*.
[8] Also ተልአከ *talaⁿəka*.

41. III=Guttural: Verbal Stems

		G-stem		D-stem		L-stem	
underived	PF	መጽአ	maṣʾa	መጽአ	maṣṣəʾa	ማጸአ	māṣəʾa
	IMPF	ይመጽእ	yəmaṣṣəʾ	ይሜጽእ	yəmeṣṣəʾ	ይማጽእ	yəmāṣṣəʾ
	SUBJ	ይምጻእ	yəmṣāʾ	ይመጽእ	yəmaṣṣəʾ	ይማጽእ	yəmāṣəʾ
	IMPV	ምጻእ	məṣāʾ	መጽእ	maṣṣəʾ	ማጽእ	māṣəʾ
	CNVRB	መጺአ	maṣiʾo	መጺአ	maṣṣiʾo	ማጺአ	māṣiʾo
	INF	መጺእ	maṣiʾ[1]	መጽአ(ት)	maṣṣəʾo(t)	ማጽአ(ት)	māṣəʾo(t)
C-stem	PF	አምጽአ	ʾamṣəʾa	አመጽአ	ʾamaṣṣəʾa		
	IMPF	ያመጽእ	yāmaṣṣəʾ	ያሜጽእ	yāmeṣṣəʾ		
	SUBJ	ያምጽእ	yāmṣəʾ	ያመጽእ	yāmaṣṣəʾ		
	IMPV	አምጽእ	ʾamṣəʾ	አመጽእ	ʾamaṣṣəʾ		
	CNVRB	አምጺአ	ʾamṣiʾo	አመጺአ	ʾamaṣṣiʾo		
	INF	አምጽአ(ት)	ʾamṣəʾo(t)	አመጽአ(ት)	ʾamaṣṣəʾo(t)		
T-stem	PF	ተመጽአ	tamaṣʾa	ተመጽአ	tamaṣṣəʾa	ተማጸአ	tamāṣəʾa
	IMPF	ይትመጻእ	yətmaṣṣāʾ	ይትሜጻእ	yətmeṣṣāʾ	ይትማጻእ	yətmāṣṣāʾ
	SUBJ	ይትመጻእ	yətmaṣāʾ	ይትመጻእ	yətmaṣṣāʾ	ይትማጻእ	yətmāṣāʾ
	IMPV	ተመጻእ	tamaṣāʾ	ተመጻእ	tamaṣṣāʾ	ተማጸእ	tamāṣāʾ
	CNVRB	ተመጺአ	tamaṣiʾo	ተመጺአ	tamaṣṣiʾo	ተማጺአ	tamāṣiʾo
	INF	ተመጽአ(ት)	tamaṣəʾo(t)	ተመጽአ(ት)	tamaṣṣəʾo(t)	ተማጽአ(ት)	tamāṣəʾo(t)
CT-stem	PF	አስተመጽአ	ʾastamaṣʾa[2]	አስተመጽአ	ʾastamaṣṣəʾa	አስተማጸአ	ʾastamāṣəʾa
	IMPF	ያስተመጽእ	yāstamaṣṣəʾ	ያስተሜጽእ	yāstameṣṣəʾ	ያስተማጽእ	yāstamāṣṣəʾ
	SUBJ	ያስተምጽእ	yāstamṣəʾ	ያስተመጽእ	yāstamaṣṣəʾ	ያስተማጽእ	yāstamāṣəʾ
	IMPV	አስተምጽእ	ʾastamṣəʾ	አስተመጽአ	ʾastamaṣṣəʾ	አስተማጽአ	ʾastamāṣəʾ
	CNVRB	አስተምጺአ	ʾastamṣiʾo	አስተመጺአ	ʾastamaṣṣiʾo	አስተማጺአ	ʾastamāṣiʾo
	INF	አስተምጽአ(ት)	ʾastamṣəʾo(t)	አስተመጽአ(ት)	ʾastamaṣṣəʾo(t)	አስተማጽአ(ት)	ʾastamāṣəʾo(t)

* The root *mṣʾ* is used for illustration only; it is not attested in all stems.
[1] Also መጺኦት *maṣiʾot*.
[2] Also አስተምጽአ *ʾastamṣəʾa*.

42. III=GUTTURAL: G-STEM PERFECT

	SG		PL	
1.c	መጻእኩ	maṣāʔku	መጻእነ	maṣāʔna
2.M	መጻእከ	maṣāʔka	መጻእክሙ	maṣāʔkəmu
2.F	መጻእኪ	maṣāʔki	መጻእክን	maṣāʔkən
3.M	መጽአ	maṣʔa	መጽኡ	maṣʔu
3.F	መጽአት	maṣʔat	መጽአ	maṣʔā

43. III=GUTTURAL: G-STEM SUBJUNCTIVE

	SG		PL	
1.c	እምጻእ	ʔəmṣāʔ	ንምጻእ	nəmṣāʔ
2.M	ትምጻእ	təmṣāʔ	ትምጽኡ	təmṣəʔu
2.F	ትምጽኢ	təmṣəʔi	ትምጽአ	təmṣəʔā
3.M	ይምጻእ	yəmṣāʔ	ይምጽኡ	yəmṣəʔu
3.F	ትምጻእ	təmṣāʔ	ይምጽአ	yəmṣəʔā

44. Q: Verbal Stems

		G-stem		L-stem	
underived	PF	ፈድፈደ	*fadfada*		
	IMPF	ይፈደፍድ	*yəfadaffəd*		
	SUBJ	ይፈድፍድ	*yəfadfəd*		
	IMPV	ፈድፍድ	*fadfəd*		
	CNVRB	ፈድፊዶ	*fadfido*		
	INF	ፈድፍዶ(ት)	*fadfədo(t)*		
C-stem	PF	አመንደበ	*ʔamandaba*		
	IMPF	ያመነድብ	*yāmanaddəb*		
	SUBJ	ያመንድብ	*yāmandəb*		
	IMPV	አመንድብ	*ʔamandəb*		
	CNVRB	አመንዲቦ	*ʔamandibo*		
	INF	አመንድቦ(ት)	*ʔamandəbo(t)*		
T-stem	PF	ተመንደበ	*tamandaba*	ተሰናሰለ	*tasanāsala*
	IMPF	ይትመነደብ	*yətmanaddab*	ይሰናሰል	*yəssanāssal*
	SUBJ	ይትመንደብ	*yətmandab*	ይሰናሰል	*yəssanāsal*
	IMPV	ተመንደብ	*tamandab*	ተሰናሰል	*tasanāsal*
	CNVRB	ተመንዲቦ	*tamandibo*	ተሰናሲሎ	*tasanāsilo*
	INF	ተመንድቦ(ት)	*tamandəbo(t)*	ተሰናስሎ(ት)	*tasanāsəlo(t)*
CT-stem	PF	አስተጠንቀቀ	*ʔastaṭankaka*	አስተጐናደየ	*ʔastagʷanādaya*
	IMPF	ያስተጠነቅቅ	*yāstaṭanakkək*	ያስተጐናዲ	*yāstagʷanāddi*[1]
	SUBJ	ያስተጠንቅቅ	*yāstaṭankək*	ያስተጐናዲ	*yāstagʷanādi*[2]
	IMPV	አስተጠንቅቅ	*ʔastaṭankək*	አስተጐናዲ	*ʔastagʷanādi*[3]
	CNVRB	አስተጠንቂቆ	*ʔastaṭankiko*	አስተጐናድዮ	*ʔastagʷanādəyo*[4]
	INF	አስተጠንቅቆ(ት)	*ʔastaṭankəko(t)*	አስተጐናድዮ(ት)	*ʔastagʷanādəyo(t)*[5]

* Different roots are cited throughout.
[1] Note the contraction of *əy* to *i* at the end; 3.M.PL is ያስተጐናድዩ *yāstagʷanāddəyu*.
[2] Note the contraction of *əy* to *i* at the end; 3.M.PL is ያስተጐናድዩ *yāstagʷanādəyu*.
[3] Note the contraction of *əy* to *i* at the end; M.PL is አስተጐናድዩ *ʔastagʷanādəyu*.
[4] Also አስተጐናዲዮ *ʔastagʷanādiyo*.
[5] Also አስተጐናዲዮ(ት) *ʔastagʷanādiyo(t)*.

45. Perfect with Pronominal Suffixes

	no suffix	1.C.SG suffix	2.M.SG suffix	2.F.SG suffix	3.M.SG suffix	3.F.SG suffix
1.C.SG	ḳatalku	–	ḳatalkuka	ḳatalkuki	ḳataləwwo	ḳataləwwā
2.M.SG	ḳatalka	ḳatalkani / ḳatalkəni	–	–	ḳatalkāhu[2]	ḳatalkāhā[4]
2.F.SG	ḳatalki	ḳatalkəni	–	–	ḳatalkəyyo	ḳatalkəyyā
3.M.SG	ḳatala	ḳatalani	ḳatalaka	ḳatalaki	ḳatalo	ḳatalā
3.F.SG	ḳatalat	ḳatalatani	ḳatalataka	ḳatalataki	ḳatalato	ḳatalatā
1.C.PL	ḳatalna	–	ḳatalnāka	ḳatalnāki	ḳatalnāhu	ḳatalnāhā
2.M.PL	ḳatalkəmu	ḳatalkəmuni	–	–	ḳatalkəməwwo	ḳatalkəməwwā[5]
2.F.PL	ḳatalkən	ḳatalkənāni[1]	–	–	ḳatalkənāhu[3]	ḳatalkənāhā[5]
3.M.PL	ḳatalu	ḳataluni	ḳataluka	ḳataluki	ḳataləwwo	ḳataləwwā
3.F.PL	ḳatalā	ḳatalāni	ḳatalāka	ḳatalāki	ḳatalāhu	ḳatalāhā

	no suffix	1.C.PL suffix	2.M.PL suffix	2.F.PL suffix	3.M.PL suffix	3.F.PL suffix
1.C.SG	ḳatalku	–	ḳatalkukəmu	ḳatalkukən	ḳatalkəwwomu	ḳatalkəwwon
2.M.SG	ḳatalka	ḳatalkana	–	–	ḳatalkomu	ḳatalkon
2.F.SG	ḳatalki	ḳatalkəna	–	–	ḳatalkəyyomu	ḳatalkəyyon
3.M.SG	ḳatala	ḳatalana	ḳatalakəmu	ḳatalakən	ḳatalomu	ḳatalon
3.F.SG	ḳatalat	ḳatalatana	ḳatalatakəmu	ḳatalatakən	ḳatalatomu	ḳatalaton
1.C.PL	ḳatalna	–	ḳatalnākəmu	ḳatalnākən	ḳatalnāhomu	ḳatalnāhon
2.M.PL	ḳatalkəmu	ḳatalkəmuna[6]	–	–	ḳatalkəməwwomu	ḳatalkəməwwon
2.F.PL	ḳatalkən	ḳatalkənāna	–	–	ḳatalkənāhomu	ḳatalkənāhon
3.M.PL	ḳatalu	ḳataluna	ḳatalukəmu	ḳatalukən	ḳataləwwomu	ḳataləwwon
3.F.PL	ḳatalā	ḳatalāna	ḳatalākəmu	ḳatalākən	ḳatalāhomu	ḳatalāhon

[1] Also ḳatalkāni.
[2] Also ḳatalko.
[3] Also ḳatalkāhu.
[4] Also ḳatalkā.
[5] Also ḳatalkāhā.
[6] Also ḳatalkāna.

46. Imperfect with Pronominal Suffixes

	no suffix	1.C.SG suffix	2.M.SG suffix	2.F.SG suffix	3.M.SG suffix	3.F.SG suffix
1.C.SG	አቀትል *ʾəḳattəl*	–	አቀትልከ *ʾəḳattələka*	አቀትልኪ *ʾəḳattəlaki*	አቀትሎ *ʾəḳattəlo*	አቀትላ *ʾəḳattəlā*
2.M.SG	ትቀትል *təḳattəl*	ትቀትለኒ *təḳattələni*	–	–	ትቀትሎ *təḳattəlo*	ትቀትላ *təḳattəlā*
2.F.SG	ትቀትሊ *təḳattəli*	ትቀትልኒ *təḳattəlini*[1]	–	–	ትቀትላዮ *təḳattəlayyo*	ትቀትላያ *təḳattəlayyā*
3.M.SG	ይቀትል *yəḳattəl*	ይቀትለኒ *yəḳattələni*	ይቀትልከ *yəḳattələka*	ይቀትልኪ *yəḳattəlaki*	ይቀትሎ *yəḳattəlo*	ይቀትላ *yəḳattəlā*
3.F.SG	ትቀትል *təḳattəl*	ትቀትለኒ *təḳattələni*	ትቀትልከ *təḳattələka*	ትቀትልኪ *təḳattəlaki*	ትቀትሎ *təḳattəlo*	ትቀትላ *təḳattəlā*
1.C.PL	ንቀትል *nəḳattəl*	–	ንቀትልከ *nəḳattələka*	ንቀትልኪ *nəḳattəlaki*	ንቀትሎ *nəḳattəlo*	ንቀትላ *nəḳattəlā*
2.M.PL	ትቀትሉ *təḳattəlu*	ትቀትሉኒ *təḳattəluni*	–	–	ትቀትላዎ *təḳattəlawwo*	ትቀትላዋ *təḳattəlawwā*
2.F.PL	ትቀትላ *təḳattəlā*	ትቀትላኒ *təḳattəlāni*	–	–	ትቀትላሁ *təḳattəlāhu*	ትቀትላሃ *təḳattəlāhā*
3.M.PL	ይቀትሉ *yəḳattəlu*	ይቀትሉኒ *yəḳattəluni*	ይቀትሉከ *yəḳattəluka*	ይቀትሉኪ *yəḳattəluki*	ይቀትላዎ *yəḳattəlawwo*	ይቀትላዋ *yəḳattəlawwā*
3.F.PL	ይቀትላ *yəḳattəlā*	ይቀትላኒ *yəḳattəlāni*	ይቀትላከ *yəḳattəlāka*	ይቀትላኪ *yəḳattəlāki*	ይቀትላሁ *yəḳattəlāhu*	ይቀትላሃ *yəḳattəlāhā*

	no suffix	1.C.PL suffix	2.M.PL suffix	2.F.PL suffix	3.M.PL suffix	3.F.PL suffix
1.C.SG	አቀትል *ʾəḳattəl*	–	አቀትልክሙ *ʾəḳattələkəmu*	አቀትልክን *ʾəḳattələkən*	አቀትሎሙ *ʾəḳattəlomu*	አቀትሎን *ʾəḳattəlon*
2.M.SG	ትቀትል *təḳattəl*	ትቀትለና *təḳattələna*	–	–	ትቀትሎሙ *təḳattəlomu*	ትቀትሎን *təḳattəlon*
2.F.SG	ትቀትሊ *təḳattəli*	ትቀትልን *təḳattəlina*[2]	–	–	ትቀትላዮሙ *təḳattəlayyomu*	ትቀትላዮን *təḳattəlayyon*
3.M.SG	ይቀትል *yəḳattəl*	ይቀትለና *yəḳattələna*	ይቀትልክሙ *yəḳattələkəmu*	ይቀትልክን *yəḳattələkən*	ይቀትሎሙ *yəḳattəlomu*	ይቀትሎን *yəḳattəlon*
3.F.SG	ትቀትል *təḳattəl*	ትቀትለና *təḳattələna*	ትቀትልክሙ *təḳattələkəmu*	ትቀትልክን *təḳattələkən*	ትቀትሎሙ *təḳattəlomu*	ትቀትሎን *təḳattəlon*
1.C.PL	ንቀትል *nəḳattəl*	–	ንቀትልክሙ *nəḳattələkəmu*	ንቀትልክን *nəḳattələkən*	ንቀትሎሙ *nəḳattəlomu*	ንቀትሎን *nəḳattəlon*
2.M.PL	ትቀትሉ *təḳattəlu*	ትቀትሉና *təḳattəluna*	–	–	ትቀትላዎሙ *təḳattəlawwomu*	ትቀትላዎን *təḳattəlawwon*
2.F.PL	ትቀትላ *təḳattəlā*	ትቀትላና *təḳattəlāna*	–	–	ትቀትላሆሙ *təḳattəlāhomu*	ትቀትላሆን *təḳattəlāhon*
3.M.PL	ይቀትሉ *yəḳattəlu*	ይቀትሉና *yəḳattəluna*	ይቀትሉክሙ *yəḳattəlukəmu*	ይቀትሉክን *yəḳattəlukən*	ይቀትላዎሙ *yəḳattəlawwomu*	ይቀትላዎን *yəḳattəlawwon*
3.F.PL	ይቀትላ *yəḳattəlā*	ይቀትላና *yəḳattəlāna*	ይቀትላክሙ *yəḳattəlākəmu*	ይቀትላክን *yəḳattəlākən*	ይቀትላሆሙ *yəḳattəlāhomu*	ይቀትላሆን *yəḳattəlāhon*

[1] Also ትቀትልኒ *təḳattəlani*.
[2] Also ትቀትልን *təḳattəlana*.

47. SUBJUNCTIVE WITH PRONOMINAL SUFFIXES

	no suffix	1.C.SG suffix	2.M.SG suffix	2.F.SG suffix	3.M.SG suffix	3.F.SG suffix
1.C.SG	ʾəḵtal	—	ʾəḵtalka	ʾəḵtalki	ʾəḵtallo	ʾəḵtallā
2.M.SG	taḵtal	taḵtalani	—	—	taḵtallo	taḵtallā
2.F.SG	taḵtali	taḵtalini[1]	—	—	taḵtalayyo	taḵtalayyā
3.M.SG	yəḵtal	yəḵtalani	yəḵtalka	yəḵtalki	yəḵtallo	yəḵtallā
3.F.SG	taḵtal	taḵtalani	taḵtalka	taḵtalki	taḵtallo	taḵtallā
1.C.PL	naḵtal	—	naḵtalka	naḵtalki	naḵtallo	naḵtallā
2.M.PL	taḵtalu	taḵtaluni	—	—	taḵtalawwo	taḵtalawwā
2.F.PL	taḵtalā	taḵtalāni	—	—	taḵtalāhu	taḵtalāhā
3.M.PL	yəḵtalu	yəḵtaluni	yəḵtaluka	yəḵtaluki	yəḵtalawwo	yəḵtalawwā
3.F.PL	yəḵtalā	yəḵtalāni	yəḵtalāka	yəḵtalāki	yəḵtalāhu	yəḵtalāhā

	no suffix	1.C.PL suffix	2.M.PL suffix	2.F.PL suffix	3.M.PL suffix	3.F.PL suffix
1.C.SG	ʾəḵtal	—	ʾəḵtalkəmu	ʾəḵtalkən	ʾəḵtallomu	ʾəḵtallon
2.M.SG	taḵtal	taḵtalana	—	—	taḵtallomu	taḵtallon
2.F.SG	taḵtali	taḵtalina[2]	—	—	taḵtalayyomu	taḵtaleyyon
3.M.SG	yəḵtel	yəḵtalana	yəḵtalkəmu	yəḵtalkən	yəḵtallomu	yəḵtallon
3.F.SG	taḵtal	taḵtalana	taḵtalkəmu	taḵtalkən	taḵtallomu	taḵtallon
1.C.PL	naḵtal	—	naḵtalkəmu	naḵtalkən	naḵtallomu	naḵtallon
2.M.PL	taḵtalu	taḵtaluna	—	—	taḵtalawwomu	taḵtalawwon
2.F.PL	taḵtalā	taḵtalāna	—	—	taḵtalāhomu	taḵtalāhon
3.M.PL	yəḵtalu	yəḵtaluna	yəḵtalukəmu	yəḵtalukan	yəḵtalawwomu	yəḵtalawwon
3.F.PL	yəḵtalā	yəḵtalāna	yəḵtalākəmu	yəḵtalākan	yəḵtalāhomu	yəḵtalāhon

[1] Also ተቅተለኒ taḵtalani.
[2] Also ተቅተለነ taḵtalana.

APPENDIX: PARSING GUIDE

When parsing a *noun*, the following morpho-syntactic information should be provided:

GENDER: masculine or feminine (only relevant for human nouns)
NUMBER: singular or plural
STATE: absolute, construct, or pronominal
CASE: non-accusative or accusative

The following examples provide samples for parsing nouns:

ወውሉደ ፡ እስራኤል ፡ ሖሩ ፡
wawəluda ʾəsrāʾel ḥoru
'The children of Israel went.' (Ex. 14:29)

ውሉደ *wəluda* masculine, plural, construct, non-accusative

ወነሥአ ፡ ኅብስተ ፡
wanaśʾa ḫəbəsta
'He took bread.' (Gen. 21:14)

ኅብስተ *ḫəbəsta* singular, absolute, accusative (ኅብስተ *ḫəbəsta* is non-human, and therefore gender is irrelevant)

When parsing a *verb*, the following morpho-syntactic information should be provided:

LEXICAL STEM: G, D, L, or Q
DERIVED STEM: Ø, C, T, or CT
FORM: perfect, imperfect, subjunctive, imperative, infinitive, or converb
PERSON: 1, 2, or 3
GENDER: masculine or feminine
NUMBER: singular or plural

All this information is required for the perfect, imperfect, subjunctive, and converb. The imperative does not require person, and the infinitive does not require person, gender, or number.
    The following examples provide samples for parsing verbs:

ያዕቆብ ፡ ባረከ ፡ ላዕለ ፡ ፈርዖን ፡
yāʿḳob bāraka lāʿla farʿon
'Jacob blessed Pharaoh.' (*History of Joseph*)

ባረከ *bāraka* underived L, perfect, 3, masculine, singular

ምንተ ፡ ገበርከ ፡
mənta gabarka
'What have you done?' (Gen. 4:10)

ገበርከ *gabarka* underived G, perfect, 2, masculine, singular

BIBLIOGRAPHY

Brockelmann, C. "Zur Kritik der traditionellen Aussprache des Äthiopischen." *Zeitschrift für Semitistik und verwandte Gebiete* 7 (1929): 205–213.

Butts, A. M. "Gəʿəz (Classical Ethiopic)." In *The Semitic Language Family*, edited by J. Huehnergard and N. Pat-El, 117–144. New York: Routledge, 2019.

Chaine, M. *Grammaire éthiopienne*. New Ed. Beirut: Imprimerie catholique, 1938.

Cohen, M. "La prononciation traditionnelle du Guèze (éthiopien classique)." *Journal asiatique* 11.17 (1921): 19–57.

Dillmann, A. *Grammatik der äthiopischen Sprache*. 1st ed. Leipzig: T. O. Weigel, 1857.

Dillmann, A. (edited and revised by C. Bezold). *Grammatik der äthiopischen Sprache*. 2nd ed. Leipzig: C. H. Tauchnitz, 1899.

Dillmann, A. (edited and revised by C. Bezold; translated by J. A. Crichton). *Ethiopic Grammar*. London: Williams & Norgate, 1907.

Gragg, G. "Geʿez (Ethiopic)." In *The Semitic Languages*, edited by R. Hetzron, 242–260. New York: Routledge, 1997.

Gragg, G. "Ge'ez (Aksum)." In *The Cambridge Encyclopedia of the World's Ancient Languages*, edited by R. D. Woodard, 427–453. Cambridge: Cambridge University Press, 2004.

Lambdin, T. O. *Introduction to Classical Ethiopic (Geʿez)*. Harvard Semitic Studies 24. Atlanta: Scholars Press, 1978.

Littmann, E. "Geʿez-Studien I–III." *Nachrichten von der königlichen Gesellschaft der Wissenschaften zu Göttingen. Philologisch-historische Klasse* 1917: 627–702; 1918: 318–339.

Makonnen Argaw. *Matériaux pour l'étude de la prononciation traditionnelle du Guèze*. Paris: Éditions Recherche sur les Civilisations, 1984.

Mittwoch, E. *Die traditionelle Aussprache des Äthiopischen*. Berlin: De Gruyter, 1926.

Praetorius, F. *Grammatica aethiopica*. Karlsruhe and Leipzig: H. Reuther, 1886.

Tropper, J. *Altäthiopisch. Grammatik des Geʿez mit Übungstexten und Glossar*. Elementa Linguarum Orientis 2. Münster: Ugarit-Verlag, 2002.

Tropper, J. and R. Hasselbach-Andee. *Classical Ethiopic. A Grammar of Geʿez*. Languages of the Ancient Near East 10. University Park: Eisenbrauns, 2021.

Ullendorff, E. *The Semitic Languages of Ethiopia. A Comparative Phonology*. London: Taylor's Foreign Press, 1955.

Voigt, R. "Classical Ethiopic (Geʿez)." In *Morphologies of Asia and Africa*, edited by A. S. Kaye, 193–210. Winona Lake: Eisenbrauns, 2007.

Weninger, S. *Gəʿəz*. Munich: Lincom Europa, 1999.

Weninger, S. "Old Ethiopic." In *The Semitic Languages. An International Handbook*, edited by S. Weninger, 1124–1151. Berlin: De Gruyter, 2011.